Introduction

This booklet is intended to be a reference guide for tutors and students about learning/teaching spelling. Some sections, especially **look, cover, write, check** are particularly useful for students. We would encourage tutors to develop handouts for them to keep from this section. We have found that by acquiring a better understanding of words, word patterns, word constructions and their own learning strategies, students become more excited, involved and interested in language work. We would hope that the work on spelling would facilitate the development of language and provide a base for continued student progress.

This booklet focuses on spelling but the importance of the content of what is being written should always be stressed.

The aim is to encourage the teacher/tutor to use the student's own written words as the basis of a spelling programme. It explains how the teacher/tutor can analyse these words, develop an individual scheme for each student and encourage appropriate strategies for learning to spell.

The Authors

Robin Millar

is the Director of the ILEA's Learning Difficulties Support Service which is the diagnostic and teaching service for adult (16+) students. Robin has also developed an extensive training programme on specific learning difficulties for teachers in adult and further education.

Cynthia Klein

has taught in Adult Literacy since 1978. For the last four years she has taught spelling and writing to adult students with specific learning difficulties through the Learning Difficulties Support Service and in both Further Education and Adult Education Institutes. She has also run training workshops in teaching spelling and in identifying and teaching students with specific learning difficulties.

> ILEA's Learning Difficulties Support Service
> 1 Gerridge Street
> London SE1
> ☎ 01–633 0053

Acknowledgements

The authors would like to acknowledge their indebtedness to several researchers and authors of spelling books *see bibliography*. They have adopted and adapted many of their ideas for this book. They would also like to thank colleagues in the ILEA Language and Literacy Unit, especially Liz Maskell, and tutors in further and adult education who provided support and advice and many patient and persevering students.

Making Sense of Spelling

Table of Contents

Introduction   3

Why Teach Spelling

Advantages Of Developing A Spelling Programme   6

Individual Analaysis Of Students' Spelling Strategies   7

The Methods They Use To Work Out And Remember Spellings   10

Attitudes To Learning   10

Strategies Used In Spelling   11

Spelling Programme

Introduction To The Spelling Programme   12

Selecting Words To Be Learned   15

Practising Spellings – LOOK, COVER, WRITE, CHECK   16

Dictations   18

Working With Older Beginning Students   20

Specific Spelling Difficulties   21
    Perception   21
    Memory   22
    Handwriting   24

Follow Up   27

Spelling Within The Classroom   28

Bibliography   30

Why Teach Spelling

Students may want to improve their spelling for many reasons. However, those with specific learning difficulties need to work on spelling because generally their writing has suffered in the following ways:

- If students cannot write automatically spelling interferes with fluent written expression. If they need to concentrate on the technical construction of words the free flow of their thoughts, ideas, vocabulary will undoubtedly suffer.

- Students will often substitute another **easier** word for the one they cannot spell. Their written sentence structure and vocabulary may appear to be weak and immature. The quality of their thinking and understanding of a topic is not adequately conveyed through their writing.

- Students may avoid writing altogether because they cannot spell many of the words they want to use.

Even when the classroom atmosphere is encouraging and supportive, many students will not write until they begin to learn to spell.

Students need to discover that making spelling errors is a necessary step in learning.

ERRORS CAN BE CORRECTED. SPELLING CAN BE LEARNED.

Advantages Of Developing A Spelling Programme

- When involved in a spelling programme, the student is encouraged to take risks in writing and to be willing to make errors.

- When students realise that their errors are needed to provide spellings, they will use more adventurous vocabulary.

- Students gain confidence in the process of writing when spelling improves.

- If you feel confident about using the methods suggested in this book then the student will gain confidence - and use the methods succesfully.

- By participating in a spelling programme, students learn more about their learning style and can apply additional strategies as tuition proceeds.

Individual Analysis Of Students' Spelling Strategies

Learning about how individual students spell

Before setting up a spelling programme it is useful to discover:

- ■　　　the types of errors they make.

- ■　　　the methods they use to work out and remember spellings.

- ■　　　the student's attitudes and feelings about spelling.

The easiest way to discover how students spell is to examine a piece of writing they have composed unaided. Ask them to write a short piece, using the words they want, not those they can already spell.

Encourage them to guess at spellings without worrying about them.
Explain that the more errors they make the easier it is to see their difficulties and to decide how to help them. Ask them to underline any words they are not sure about to see if they can spot and/or correct their own errors.

Types of errors made

Part of learning to spell is becoming aware of common letter patterns, their frequency and likelihood of usage (See Bibliography Peters 1975 and Frith 1980). When looking at writing look for how much linguistic competence has been acquired. As a rough guide sort the errors into these four categories. Students may make errors of all types but we have found it useful to identify the most common and frequent ones.

- Logical Phonetic Alternatives. This means that most of the errors are close to spelling precedent and correspond to common English letter patterns. Example: **serched** for searched, **frend** for friend, **terned** for turned. A student whose errors are mainly of this type is well on the way to learning to spell.

- Generalisation Problems. Errors of this type show that a student has not acquired an awareness of common **rules** or generalisations. Example: **studys** for studies, **shoping** for shopping, **shage** for shaggy.

- Transposition of significant letters or syllables. Errors of this type, when they are frequent, indicate that a student has difficulty sequencing sounds or letter patterns. Example: **frist** for first, **specail** for special, **flim** for film, **vioce** for voice, **interput** for interupt.

- Omission or confusion of significant sounds or syllables. If errors of this type are common, the student may have difficulty discriminating sounds and/or remembering sound/symbol correlations. Example: **sreet** for street, **capalled** for collapsed, **axcely** for actually, **chunce** for chance; **imediale** for immediately.

Samples of students' writing

The following examples are taken from the writing of two different students. Both were fluent readers and not beginning writers. Each was given the dictation below and asked to **guess** at how the words were spelt, even if they had never written them before. These examples illustrate different approaches and possible weaknesses that students may have.

"One day, as I was walking down Bridge Street, I heard the sound of trotting. I turned and saw behind me the shaggy dark hair of a frightened little horse. I searched in my pockets for an apple from my dinner to give him. 'I know where you should be', I said. So I removed the belt of my raincoat and tied it around his neck and led him back. I opened the gate, and with satisfaction he galloped into his field. I was certainly very happy that now he was safe, away from the noisy and dangerous traffic".

Weak visual perception

This student is a phonetic speller. Almost all words are readable, and lack visual elements to make them accurate. Note the spelling of **bark** for **dark** *continued letter reversal*.

Illustration 1

Weak auditory perception

This student has a more difficult time making guesses at words. Because the recall of the sounds of the letters is a problem, some words prove difficult to decipher **frited** for frightened, **terd** for turned. Significant sounds are often missing the **r** in heard, **pockes** for pockets, **tie** for tied. The student attempts to remember words visually but can easily mis-sequence letters **blit** for belt. If students have a poor visual memory for the word they may not be able to attempt more than the first one or two letters **ap** for apple.

Illustration 2

9

The Methods They Use To Work Out And Remember Spellings.

Many students are not aware that writing is an on–going process and that it is acceptable, even beneficial to make mistakes. They do not realise that good writers make rough drafts, edit and proof read. Instead, they believe a piece of writing should be perfect first time.

If asked to check their writing can they recognise errors? i.e. have they got a good visual image of a word? Some people know when they have spelt a word wrong, but cannot correct it. Others cannot identify misspelt words.

Ask the student what they do when they can't spell a word.

Do they:

- ask someone?

- use a dictionary?

- use another, easier word instead?

- try to learn words by themselves? If so, how do they set about it? Are they familiar with techniques that can be used to learn words?

Often students say of their school experience, *"Teachers used to tell me to go and learn the words, but they didn't tell me how"*.

Many students are inconsistent spellers and may spell a word three different ways on the same page. They may have difficulty seeing their errors or remembering when it **looks right**. Often they say *"I just can't remember spellings"*. They frequently have **good days** and **bad days**. These students are more usefully seen as **quick forgetters** rather than slow learners.

Attitudes To Learning

In order to find out about the students' experiences and attitudes towards spelling discuss these with them. It is important to know how they feel about writing and spelling. For instance do they avoid writing because of spelling difficulties?

It is also important to ask what they need to spell and what they would like to able to spell. Some are held back from applying for jobs they would like to do: others feel humiliated because they cannot even write a note, others are frustrated because they would like to pursue a course of study and cannot cope with the writing requirements.

This information is extremely valuable in setting up a relevant spelling programme. It is also important to know about motivation. Are they willing to practice spellings between sessions? Are they willing to write in order to learn to spell?

Strategies Used In Spelling

Students are often puzzled by the difficulties they have in spelling even though they are competent readers. In many instances they have been previously told to *"go away and read more and your spelling will improve !"* When this method does not work, they begin to feel incompetent and frustrated.

Considerable discussion may be needed so that students understand why they have learned one language skill and not another.

Quite simply, when students have become independent readers they no longer look closely at what they read. In fact, 'most readers predict as they read from minimal information on the page, and the better the readers, the less closely they look at what is on the page'. (Peters, p.7. see bibliography) In order to remember the spelling of words, we need to look closely at them and remember all the parts not just the general configuration.

Spelling is a sub skill of writing. This skill is dependent upon total recall of words with a high reliance on visual memory. Therefore, to spell competently we need to remember all the letters of the words in correct sequence. As writers we use all our sensory/perceptual systems (visual/auditory/motor) to cross check spelling attempts.

For example, if you ask good spellers to spell a word, they will usually need to write the word and then check it to see if it **looks right**. To remember a word we need **an adequate memory of how it feels to write it** and **an adequate picture of how it looks**.

Visualising can be taught and its positive effects on spelling have been verified by research. However, many students need to be taught visualising and students may also need help in improving handwriting skills.

Spelling Programme

Introduction To The Spelling Programme

Students need to understand several things before beginning a spelling programme:

- that because they have had difficulties remembering spellings in the past, it is necessary to have an accurate diagnosis by the tutor or learning support staff.

- that there are differences between spelling and reading. *"Why can I read but can't spell?"* (see 'Strategies used in Spelling')

- that there are misconceptions about how good spellers spell. Students often do not realise that good spellers use a variety of strategies to learn words. Good spellers apply many alternative ways of learning words without being told how to do it. Tuition is smoother when students accept that **any strategies that they do use are acceptable.**

- that they need to practice spellings correctly. Discussion about long-term and short-term memory and how they work is useful *(see page 22)* Practicing spelling at prescribed intervals will help get the words into long term memory where they are more likely to be remembered automatically.

- that learning all the spellings every week may prove hard because of specific difficulties. This is why reinforcing dictations are provided each week. The student can then feel more secure that the spellings will not be forgotten.

- that students who find it difficult to acquire spellings will not learn from learning spelling rules or general patterns which they merely practice as an exercise. There is a vast difference between understanding, remembering and applying. Students may be able to do an exercise on spelling such as **i** before **e** words or **tion** endings but this does not mean they will be able to remember and use these letter patterns appropriately in their writing.

An effective spelling programme needs to be:

Meaningful:related to students own need to spell and based on words they use or want to use in their free writing. This is particularly important for anyone with short term memory difficulties.

Individualised: words should be selected, grouped and broken up to facilitate the particular student's learning – e.,g. **phonics** will not work with students who have auditory perceptual difficulties.

Multi–Sensory: using all the senses to reinforce each other in learning and emphasising the student's strengths.

Structured: to minimise confusion of word patterns, to develop and build spelling vocabulary that students can use in their writing and to enable adequate reinforcement and review of learned spelling so that they do not **lose** them.

Slow with repetition: keep to small chunks of learning. Students cannot learn letter patterns, rules or letter combinations if too many are introduced at once. Limit the number of different patterns taught in each lesson.

For the spelling programme to be effective, the students must produce a new piece of writing each week from which spellings are selected to be learned. Encourage the students to write without worrying about spellings and to use words they may not know how to spell. Students should attempt the desired word if possible, even if only the initial letter(s), so that they will remember the intended word when reading it back.

Students are generally more willing to risk making mistakes if they understand the notion of a **rough draft** which is revised before writing the final draft.

When going over the rough draft with the student, provide the correct spelling and select which spellings are to be learned for the next week. Do not ignore errors, but make it clear that only a limited number can be learned each week.

We suggest the following ideas for encouraging and developing student writing:

- Avoid the use of dictionaries for spelling purposes. Students with specific difficulties, particularly auditory perceptual ones, find using a dictionary frustrating, time consuming and generally unrewarding.

- Ask the students to write on loose paper rather than exercise books. This helps to develop the idea of a **rough draft**. Writing on one side of the paper only also helps students with short term memory difficulties, as they can then see the continuity of their writing.

- When possible, encourage experienced students to take a course with a writing component if they are not doing so already. The weekly piece of free writing can then be either an assignment from the course or expanded from the course work. The weekly writing is then more meaningful and the student develops written expression, spelling vocabulary and writing skills to the appropriate level.

Selecting Words To Be Learned

Each week the tutor's responsibilty is:

■   to make up a list of **APPROPRIATE** words to be learned and to test them.

■   to compile a list of learned words for dictation the following week.

Group errors to find patterns:

     Rules – baby – babies, company – companies

     Letter patterns – feet, beet, sweet

     Suffixes prefixes – dis – connect, dis – obey

     Select words – maximum of 10 –12 with the student on the basis of:

■   errors close to correct spelling or student already knows another word with similar letter pattern.

■   frequency of usage by student.

■   words the student is highly motivated to learn.

■   common words – **this, there, which, they**.

■   words with common patterns. *It is important to build the student's awareness of these.*

        – **ight** words
        – **ear** words
        – **tion** suffix etc.

Link words with others of identical visual patterns:

       come – home – some
       bear – beard – heard
       bead – head – instead

or with similar roots prefixes or suffixes.

       gener   **ally**
       fin   **ally**
       natur   **ally**

Never present words in the same week with confusing sound patterns or letter sequences.

    e.g.   –   **ere and ear words** *hear, here*
                 –   **sion and tion**
                 –   **form and from**
                 –   **salt and flat**

Practising Spellings

It would be useful to divide the page into columns *see example below*.

Discuss with the student the words that are to be learned and recommend a suitable method for remembering them. Write each word correctly or make sure that the student has a correct copy of it in column one. Explain to students that they should:

LOOK at the word, noting the area of particular difficulty and say it aloud. Close their eyes and try to visualise it.

COVER the word. Say it aloud.

WRITE the word in column 2. Say it as they write it.

CHECK that the word is correct. If not, copy the correct spelling above or near the original, paying attention to any mistakes. **If a mistake has been made it is important to correct it by writing the whole word again not just by changing or adding letters. The experience of writing the whole word is important.**

Next day, repeat the process and spell each word again in column 3.

Two or three days later, repeat the process and spell the words in column 4.

1.	2.	3.	4.
Shake	Shake	Shake	Shacke X Shake
Shaking	Shaking	Shaking	Shaking
taking	taking	taking	taking
allow	allow	allow	allow
Coward	Coward	Coward	Coward
Particular	Particular	particular	Particular
Particularly	Particularly	Particularly	Particular
article	article	artical X article	Article
rainy	rainy	Rainy	rainy
wait await awaiting	Wait await awaiting	Wait await awaiting	Wait await awaiting

Emphasize the following points:

■ the need to visualise or make an image of a word to remember how it looks. In order to remember spellings copying is largely a waste of time because it does not force us to pay attention to the **look** of the word. To remember spellings we need a visual image of a word.

■ This approach uses all the senses to help remember the word by linking the look, the sound and the feeling of writing the word.

■ This method works. It will work in spite of past failures.

■ We need to be excited and enthusiastic about words. Thinking about, looking at and noticing more words generates enthusiasm and encourages risk taking when writing.

Have They Learned The Words On The Spelling List?

■ Each word is dictated to the student.

■ The student repeats the word aloud and then writes it.

■ The student spells the written word orally.

■ If a word has an error, ask the student to find it e.g. say *"Something's missing from that word. Can you find it?"* If the error is not easily identifed do not let the student flounder. Display the correct spelling, compare it to the copy and discuss differences.

■ The student looks at the word again and writes it correctly from memory. This word is added to the next week's spelling list. During the initial weeks of tuition you may need to emphasize that the process takes time. Point out any progress made in recognising and correcting errors. Reminders about the method may be necessary in the early stages.

■ A small exercise book is useful for keeping spellings in one place. As the weeks progress words learned can be transferred to a personal dictionary.

Dictations

Sentences should be constructed from words the students have demonstrated they know. The purpose of dictation is to give the students practice in writing the learned words in context. More than one spelling word may be incorporated into each sentence. About five sentences each week should be given.

- Dictate the sentence.

- The student repeats the sentence and then writes it from memory. If the sentence is too long it may need to be divided into chunks.

- The student should proof read the sentence immediately and if possible correct any errors.

- Point out any errors that have not been noticed. The student should be encouraged to correct them.

- If an error is not corrected show the correct version and ask the student to write it correctly from memory.

- Continue this process with each sentence.

Dictations help us to identify:

- words the student finds hard to learn.

- easily confused sounds or sequences.

- strategies used to remember words.

Samples of dictation

Literacy Student

illustration 3

① The idea was to cure her sight.
② They closed a deal on the seal coat
③ what night were you there?.
④ We come closer to the treasure and sight a birth sight
⑤ We was sure the lady wanted a clean suit
⑥ The moon looked little on that wintery night.

18

'O' Level Student

This student is aware of the difficulties she has with certain words and will try to attempt several spellings of them. Like many students with specific difficulties, even when she arrives at the correct spellings she cannot always identify them. However, the dictations allow her to attempt words she has practised and encourage her to increase her ability to predict where her errors lie.

It should also be noted that if a student **forgets** an old spelling and cannot easily correct mistakes, that spelling is added to a current list for review and practise.

illustration 4

Working With Older Beginnning Students

With students who are beginning readers and/or writers, the spelling programme can still be put into effect by building on language experience techniques.

Examples:

- One student was a van driver and unable to leave a note to say he had called. We started on simple sequences relating to the student's work and took words from sentences which were then learned by the **look, cover, write, check** method.

Examples of words learned:

> **drive, driver, live**
> **deliver, delivery**
> **back, sack**
> **pack, package**

Sentences based on these words were later dictated and each week we expanded on the sentence until we were able to experiment with sentences: e.g. *"I tried to deliver a package on Monday"*.

- One student had such difficulty with spelling that he refused to write at all. In this case a volunteer was used who prepared the ground for a piece of writing with the student through discussion. The student dictated what he wanted written to the volunteer who acted as a scribe. Then the student read the piece of writing. Words were chosen from it for the student to learn. Once the student had acquired a basic writing vocabulary he was enouraged to start writing on his own. Again, as he learned enough of the spellings his own sentences were dictated back to him.

It is helpful with beginners and non–writers to focus the writing on one subject, e.g. work, a hobby, autobiography and to develop a large number of high use and consistent words. This allows adequate reinforcement and practice and helps students master enough words on one subject to be able to write something meaningful fairly quickly. This increases motivation and confidence.

Those who need more strategies for remembering

For many students the **Look, Cover, Write, Check** method is sufficient to remember the majority of spellings. However, some especially those with specific spelling difficulties, will need additional memory aids to remember spellings.

Specific Spelling Difficulties

Perception

The aim of this book is not to present detailed descriptions of perception or perceptual difficulties but some understanding of these is helpful for both tutors and students. It is important for the tutor and student to recognise the perceptual processes that we use when learning spellings. Some people have particular weaknesses in auditory or visual perception and/or memory and need to understand these weaknesses in order to adopt successful strategies for learning.

It is important to stress that this does not mean difficulties in seeing or hearing. The student may have perfectly adequate vision and hearing. Perception has to do with the ability to process the information received in order to discriminate, remember and recall fine differences in sounds or letters.

Perceptual Difficulties

■ **Visual Perception**. People with poor visual perception may find remembering the letters difficult (i.e. words are spelt phonetically). They may confuse the direction of certain letters e.g. **b/d**, **p/q**, **m/w**, **n/u**, **t/f**. This visual confusion remains even when the student is a competent writer.

■ **Auditory Perception**. People with poor auditory perception may find remembering the sound or patterns of sounds difficult. Significant sounds in words may be omitted or confused. Often they attempt to remember the word visually but cannot get the sequence correct e.g. **gril** for girl, **faimly** for family. Sounds which prove difficult are blends **gr**, **br**, **fl**, or unaccented syllables.

■ **Motor difficulties** *difficulties associated with movement*. These may be associated with weak perception – *see above*.

People with motor difficulties may have trouble with:

■ forming or reproducing letters and/or words.

■ remembering direction.

■ manipulating the writing implement.

■ joining letters.

They may have general handwriting difficulties, visual tracking problems or overall problems planning their written work.

Memory

Students may need to understand the difference between long term memory and short term memory in order to understand why they have continuing spelling difficulties. We store information we want to remember in our long term memory. Highly meaningful information, like experiences or events in our lives, is easily retrieved from the long term memory. Other information may be less easy to retrieve. However, in order to spell fluently, we need to remember and retrieve words from our long term memories.

Our short term memory is used to recall information immediately after we have attended to it. For example we use short term memory to recall a telephone number long enough to dial, or to remember a passage we have read. Some students may have difficulty holding more than two or three letters in their short term memory in order to write them down. Even then, these students may not remember the letters or the order of them unless they are consciously memorising them.

If the memorisation is meaningful, then we can store the information in our long term memory, and if it is organised effectively, we can retrieve it when we want to.

In order to write fluently we need to know how words are spelt so we do not have to think about it. If we only copy words we are using our short term memory for a few letters at a time, just long enough to write the word down. However, with conscious practice which is relevant and organised, we can permanently remember and retrieve words, even if our short term memories are limited.

Getting words into long term memory takes time and we have limits as to how much we can memorise at a time. Therefore, students should understand why they should not be expected to learn more than ten words per week and should not try to learn more than this limit.

The following approaches may be useful

General memory aids which any individual student may find useful.

- Teaching students to beat out syllables and then write them as they say them.

- Highlighting words with coloured pens. This can be useful to help students focus on the bit of the word they are misspelling.

- Saying the names of the letters *letter spelling* in rhythm. This is useful for confusing endings such as: **cial/ght/**etc.

- Understanding the derivation of words:

  television: **tele** means far – **vis** means see.

- Indicating the language basis e.g. chemical comes from Greek.

Memory aid for students with auditory perceptual difficulties

- Finding words within words. This may need to be demonstrated to the student.

  Example: **Cap/a/city** for capacity
  we/at/her for weather

- Reinforcing spellings by providing additional words of similar letter patterns:

  please - ease - disease
  sound - found - round

Memory aid for students with visual memory difficulties

- by exaggerating pronunciation of words: **be/ca/use** for because of the student is advised to **say it funny** as they write it.

- understanding the structure of words, e.g. morphemes, root words, suffixes, prefixes, etc.

- providing format for building on root words: e.g. appoint, disappoint, disappointment, disappointed, etc.

Handwriting

If students are having difficulty controlling their handwriting or print because their handwriting is **too messy** this may suggest that motor difficulties are interfering with their writing. Note whether the student is having problems with letter formation, including letter reversals **raddit** for rabbit.

Another handwriting problem may be perseveration *when the hand cannot stop* e.g. **beginining** for beginning, **openened** for opened. Some students will also say that their *hand takes over* and for example makes a **g** when they want to make an **a**.

Finally, some students have learned to make their writing, or at least certain words or letters, illegible in order to hide spelling mistakes. Usually they will admit to this if asked.

Importance of handwriting in learning to spell

The **motor** aspect of spelling is handwriting. The motor memory or muscle memory is one of our strongest memories. Once a motor skill is learned, for example bike riding, it is very difficult to forget. This is one reason why consistently misspelled words are difficult to unlearn.

When a writer prints, the letters are isolated and the hand has no **memory for how it feels** to produce certain patterns of letters. By joining up more letters the chance of correctly remembering a word is increased because, not only visual, but also his motor memory is being tapped.

Many students continue to print because they have never been taught to join their writing. A highly motivated student, who has no physical disability, can learn to write fluently in a matter of months. Other students continue to print because they have been told in the past that their joined writing was too messy. These students need to be encouraged to attempt a cursive style now that they are adults and have better fine motor control.

Ways to teach joined up writing

Observe and discuss with students their current writing style. Note such things as:

paper position – pen grip – left/right handedness and whether any one of these is interfering with fluency. Often students are not aware of alternate and possibly more comfortable ways of holding a pen or angling the paper.

Most students are eager to improve the quality of their handwriting and will willingly experiment with a variety of styles and pens.

General advice

Encourage students to experiment with:

- signature writing

- a variety of implements:
  pen – pencils – calligraphy pens – ball point – fountain/cartridge – roller ball pens – felt tips etc.

- relaxation exercises to un–tense hand muscles.

- exercises to strengthen hand muscles, such as squeezing a rubber ball – manipulating clay – kneading bread.

- writing common patterns to get the flow of joining up letters. **uuu, lll, mmm, ccc**

- calligraphy styles via books, magazines.

Do not expect the student to join up all letters only those which are easily grouped. e.g. **tion**, or, **ell**

If students find they can connect certain letter combinations more easily than others encourage them to join up letters wherever it feels **natural**.

Some students find this possible within their writing, others may need to begin by learning joined up writing only on their spelling words. Students might only be expected to join up the words which they are practising for that week.

Students may need specific instruction on where to start a letter and where to finish it. Exercises which demonstrate the construction and direction of how letters are connected can be useful. It may be necessary to discuss, in detail, when construction problems are interfering with fluency. Style may be awkward and messy so encouragement to practice is needed until the production of letters is fluent and automatic.

Other activities to support handwriting

- suggest that students read one another's writing.

- students can be encouraged to produce something for publication. Start with initial drafts and show them that everyone uses different styles of handwriting for different purposes. Rough outline – 2nd draft – proof reading – re–draft – finished work.

- students may be interested in calligraphy if so develop a series of lessons.

- work on reversals.

Some students consistently confuse, reverse, or rotate certain letters and/or numbers, e.g. **b/d – p/q – g/9 – m/w – z/2 – 5/s**. Learning to join up letters should help to reduce these confusions. The construction of each letter in connected script differs and the motor memory should reduce the visual confusions.

Follow Up

Why isn't your student learning?

It is essential for the confidence of both the student and the tutor that the spellings are learnt successfully. If the student is not learning them it is very important to find why not.

Perhaps the student is not following the method correctly.

Students need to understand the reasons for each step of the method. Often they do not realise the importance of following all the steps, have their own ideas about how to learn spellings or misunderstand instructions. The most usual reasons for failure are:

Covering: they may not be adequately covering the word before writing it. They may be peeping at the word as they write it. By using visual cues they fail to get practice in retaining the image of the word.

Checking: the students may not be checking back adequately, letter for letter. They may think they already know it, or may have difficulty seeing errors.

Visualising or making an image: students may put emphasis on testing rather than visualising or making an image and may either try to memorise the whole list of words or get someone else to test them orally. Again they fail to practice.

Practising at prescribed intervals: students may fill in all the columns of spellings just before the session.

Perhaps the student may be having specific difficulties which need to be worked on.

Tracking: students may telescope or lose parts of words – **avaible** for available – or missequence parts of words –**orangisation** for organisation.

In this case students need lots of practice with the tutor in breaking words up and saying the word in the corresponding bits while writing it. This is especially important if the students are to handle multisyllabic words.

Proof reading: students may miscopy or misspell words and have difficulty seeing errors. They need practice in checking the word back in sections with attention to the sequencing of letters.

Retaining spellings once learned: this indicates that the students are either not following the method accurately or not getting enough practice and review. It is important to make sure that they are producing regular free writing using the spellings. Some students with severe difficulties, need extra reinforcement and review.

If students find learning spellings particularly difficult after checking all the above possibilities, try using:

- plastic or magnetic letters – to reinforce letter patterns take away initial letters to make new words – night, right, fight.

- Fernald method – using tracing for motor reinforcement *see bibliography for more details*.

- Edith Norrie Letter Case *see bibliography*.

Spelling Within the Classroom

One of the main problems for tutors in using an individualised spelling approach with students is how to make time for this within the framework of a group teaching situation. Initially you may need considerable time to explain the spelling method to the students and to set up the programme. They need much less time once they understand the method. Spellings and dictations can be practised in a small group with the tutor giving each student a word or sentence in turn. Students who are competent readers can work in pairs giving each other their dictations (which have been written out). Go over the sentences with the students first to make sure they can read all the words. They can then help each other check the words, developing proof reading skills.

They can also work in pairs or small groups to develop a piece of writing, for instance after a large group discussion, leaving the tutor to work individually with the students who need it. As regular free writing is an integral part of the spelling programme some time each session should be devoted to it, again leaving the tutor free for individual work with students. Once students stop worrying about correct spelling they will write more freely and independently. Each student can then be helped to select words for their spelling lists while the other are writing.

If there are two teachers in a class, organise the students so that one teacher works with one, two or three students on their spelling list whilst the other works with the rest of the group. Explain to the whole group that this is the way the class is set up. Discuss this organisation with the class and explain that this approach will enable everyone to get more concentrated help as needed. This reduces the possibility of students feeling left out or not special.

If you or the students are anxious that students receiving specific tuition in spelling are missing out on the group work, ask other students within the larger group to take on the task of explaining to them what they have missed. This encourages more student participation in addition to giving valuable practice in recalling, explaining and sequencing.

The most important points to remember in developing individual tuition within a group are:

- The need for flexibility in relation to the individual needs of the students in the class. It is more relevant for a student to spend 15–20 minutes working on specific tasks related to their needs than to spend two hours not meeting these specific needs.

- The responsibility and participation of the students needs to be encouraged. Once large and small groups and working in pairs has been established only minimal supervision is needed. Students also need to develop a sense of responsibility for and control over their work. Tutors often need to be facilitators as much as teachers.

- Group work does not mean that everyone has to do the same things. It should rather be seen as a starting point from which individual students, pairs and small groups can develop in different ways and at different levels.

- Finally, rethinking the idea of a fixed class time may open up new options. For instance, in a two or three hour time slot students could come for staggered periods of time for spelling/learning support rather than for a class. Students might only come for 30–45 minutes to do their spellings; others might stay for the whole session, forming informal groups to work on their writing or for extra tuition on specific and writing problems. We have found this kind of session is particularly useful for students who also attend other classes which are more content orientated. They can then work on spelling and developing writing generated by the other class.

The form of such a learning support session might vary from week to week and from group to group depending on specific student needs and tutor preferences. Sometimes it might consist of mainly individual or pairs work, at other times it might be more group orientated with only some time spent on individual spellings.

Tutors and students need to experiment with other forms, methods and approaches which might work for them.

A successful formula is one which meets the specific needs of all the students.

Bibliography

Spelling

Alpha to Omega.
HORNSBY Beve & SHEAR Frula.
Heinemann. 1980.
ISBN 0 435 10382 2

Catchwords. Ideas for Teaching Spelling.
CRIPPS, Charles.
Harcourt Brace Jovanovich Group, Sydney. 1978.
ISBN 0 7295 0184 1

Children and Parents and Spellling
JEFFS, Alvin.
Home and School Council (Sheffield)
ISBN 0 901181 53 6

Cognitive Processes in Spelling.
FRITH, Uta.
Academic Press. 1980.
ISBN 0 12 268662 4

Diagnostic and Remedial Spelling Manual.
PETERS, M.
Macmillan Ed. 1975.
ISBN 0 333 15554 8

Get it Right.
TEMPLE, Michael.
John Murray. 1978.
ISBN 0 7195 3507 7

Gnosis. 5.
D.C.L.D. Publishing. October. 1984.
D.C.L.D. Ebury Teachers' Centre
Sutherland Street SW1 4LH

Gnosis. 6.
D.C.L.D. Publishing. April. 1985.
D.C.L.D. Ebury Teachers' Centre
Sutherland Street SW1 4LH

Helping Adults to Spell.
MOORHOUSE, Catherine.
ALBSU Publications.
from: AdultLiteracyandBasic SkillsUnit, Kingsbourne
House,High Holborn
London. W.C.1.
ALBSU has produced a number of materials for stimulating writing.

How to Spell and Punctuate
LAWLEY, A.H.&LAWLEY,Marian.
University Tutorial Press. 1987.
ISBN 0 7231 0829 3

Learning to Spell. A resource Book for Teachers.
TODD, Joyce.
Basil Blackwell. 1982.
ISBN 0 631 13198 1

Logical Spelling.
ALLAN, B.V.
Collins. 1977.
ISBN 0 0031 4316 3

Remedial Techniques in Basic School Subjects
FERNALD, G.M.
McGraw (1943)
(Out of Print)

Signposts to Spelling.
POLLOCK, Joy.
Heinemann Educational Books, 1978.
ISBN 0 435 10686 4

Spelling Programmes (1978).
B.B.C. Broadcasting Support Services.

Success in Spelling.
PETER, M.
Cambridge Institute of Education. 1970.
(Out of print)

The Edith Norrie Letter Case
from *Helen Arkell Dyslexia Centre*
14 Crondace Road, London SW6

Handwriting

Improve your Handwriting.
BOULT, Trevor. & DOUGLAS, Thomas.
Edward Arnold.
ISBN 0 7131 7376 9

Handwriting Activities.
BARNARD, Thomas.
Ward Lock Educational. Basic Skills Series.
ISBN (Book 1) 0 7062 3934 2
ISBN (Book 2) 0 7062 3935 0

Teach Yourself Handwriting.
SASSOON & BRIEM.
Hodder and Stoughton. 1985.
ISBN 0 340 32159 8

Setting Out Word Bank and Handwriting.
RIDGEWAY, Bill.
Edward Arnold.
ISBN 0 7131 0490 2

The Development of Handwriting Skills.
JARMAN, Christopher.
Basil Blackwell.
ISBN 0 631 19230 1

The Practical Guide to Children's Handwriting.
SASSOON, Rosemary.
Thames and Hudson.
ISBN 0 500 27314 6

Writing is for Reading.
TAYLOR, Jane.
14 Dora Road, London S.W.19.

Stimulating and Developing Writing

Conversations with Strangers.
SHARPNEL GARDNER, Sue.
ISBN 0 906 509 548
from: AdultLiteracyandBasic SkillsUnit, Kingsbourne House,High Holborn
London. W.C.1.
ALBSU has produced a number of materials for stimulating writing.

Learning from Experience.
MACE, Jane.
Broadcasting Support Services
252 Western Avenue, London. W.3.
ISBN 0 906 965 02 0

Stimulating Writing.
SWINNEY, Janet.
Wages to Windscale
Friends Centre Brighton.

Writing and Spelling.
MOORHOUSE, Catherine.
Handbook. BBC Publications 1979.
ISBN 0 563 16292 9

Opening Times
The Gatehouse Project
St Luke's, Sawley Road
Miles Platting, Manchester, M1 3LY